PUFFIN BOOKS

The Mighty Slide

This story is one I've not told before;
I think I might call it The Boiler-Room Door,
Or The Beast from Below, or Stan in a Sweat;
But one thing's for sure – it's the scariest yet!

Here, in verse, are stories of a mighty slide, a man who fought crocodiles, a girl who doubled, a couple of baby skinners and a thing that lived under a school; a wonderful collection from the author of *Please Mrs Butler*, *Woof!* and *Happy Families*, with delightful pictures by Charlotte Voake.

The Mighty Slide

Stories in Verse by Allan Ahlberg

Illustrated by Charlotte Voake

PUFFIN BOOKS

PUFFIN BOOKS

Published by the Penguin Group
Penguin Books Ltd, 80 Strand, London WC2R 0RL, England
Penguin Putnam Inc., 375 Hudson Street, New York, New York 10014, USA
Penguin Books Australia Ltd, Ringwood, Victoria, Australia
Penguin Books Canada Ltd, 10 Alcorn Avenue, Toronto, Ontario, Canada M4V 3B2
Penguin Books India (P) Ltd, 11 Community Centre, Panchsheel Park, New Delhi – 110 017, India
Penguin Books (NZ) Ltd, Cnr Rosedale and Airborne Roads, Albany, Auckland, New Zealand
Penguin Books (South Africa) (Pty) Ltd, 24 Sturdee Avenue, Rosebank 2196 South Africa

Penguin Books Ltd, Registered Offices: 80 Strand, London WC2R 0RL, England

www.penguin.com

First published by Viking 1988
Published in Puffin Books 1989
12

Text copyright © Allan Ahlberg, 1988
Illustrations copyright © Charlotte Voake, 1988
Consultant Designer: Douglas Martin
All rights reserved

Printed in England by Clays Ltd, St Ives plc

Except in the United States of America, this book is sold subject
to the condition that it shall not, by way of trade or otherwise, be lent,
re-sold, hired out, or otherwise circulated without the publisher's
prior consent in any form of binding or cover other than that in
which it is published and without a similar condition including this
condition being imposed on the subsequent purchaser

Contents

The Mighty Slide

The snow has fallen in the night.
The temperature's exactly right.
The playground's ready, white and wide;
Just waiting for the mighty slide.

The first to arrive is Denis Dunne.
He takes a little stuttering run.
Sideways he slides across the snow;
He moves about a yard or so,
With knees just bent and arms out wide;
And marks the beginning of the slide.

Then Martin Bannister appears,
His collar up around his ears,
His zipper zipped, his laces tied,
And follows Denis down the slide.
The snow foams up around their feet,
And melts, too, in the friction's heat.
It changes once, it changes twice:
Snow to water; water to ice.

Now others arrive: the Fisher twins
And Alice Price. A queue begins.
The slide grows longer, front and back,
Like a giant high-speed snail's track.
And flatter and greyer and glassier, too;
And as it grows, so does the queue.
Each waits in line and slides and then
Runs round and waits and slides again.

And little is said and nothing is planned,
As more and more children take a hand
(Or a foot, if you like) in the slide's construction.
They work without wages and minus instruction.
Like a team of cleaners to and fro
With clever feet they polish the snow.
Like a temporary tribe in wintry weather,
They blow on their gloves and pull together.

10

A dozen children, maybe more,
All skidding on the frozen floor.
The brave, like bulls, just charge the ice,
And one of these is Alice Price;
Her red scarf flying in the breeze,
You'd think she had a pair of skis.
Others approach more cautiously;
Denis for one (though he wouldn't agree).
His wobbly style is unmistakable:
The sign of a boy who knows he's breakable.

And now the slide is really growing,
And the rhythm of the queue is flowing.
Some keep a place or wait for a friend,
Some dive in the snow when they reach the end,
Some slide and pretend to be terrified,
Some stand in the queue and *never* slide.

There are children with bags and children without,
As they roll the silver carpet out;
And some in pairs and some in a bunch,
And one or two *eating*: an early lunch.
There's flying hair and frozen feet,
And big and little, and scruffy and neat.
There's shouting and shoving: 'Watch this!' 'Watch me!'
'I'm floating!' 'I'm falling!' 'Oh, Mother!' 'Wheee!'
And all the while from the frosty ground
That indescribable *sliding* sound.
Yes, snow's a pleasure and no mistake,
But the slide is the icing on the cake.

'If we knocked that wall down, moved that shed,
We could slide for miles!' the children said.
'If we knocked it *all* down – wallop – bop –
We could slide for ever and never stop!'
An icy ribbon tidily curled
In a giant circle round the world.

The slide by now is forty feet long,
And a number of things have begun to go wrong.
The queue stretches back to the playground gate;
Certain boys find it hard to wait.
While tough boys like Hoskins or Kenny Burns
Are simply not *used* to taking turns.
Like pockets of chaos or bits of sin,
They break up the queue and muscle in.

And all the time the slide gets slicker,
And the sliders slide along it quicker.
The quickest by far is Frankie Slater:
'When I grow up I'll be a skater!'
The craziest? Well, Colin Whittle;
He thinks the boy in front is a skittle.
There are bumps and bruises, bets and dares,
Cries, collisions, pile-ups, *prayers*!

But even worse than damaged kids,
The slide itself is on the skids.
The feet that brought it to perfection
Are pushing it now in a different direction.
For everything changes, that much is true;
And a part of the playground is poking through.

'It's wearing away!' 'It's wearing out!'
'We need more snow!' the children shout.
At which point Hoskins quietly swears,
And – minus the coat he never wears –
Raises his hand like a traffic cop
And calls on his fellow sliders to stop.

Then straight away from the ranks of the queue
Step Denis and Martin and Alice, too.
With no one to tell them and no one to ask,
They tackle the urgent chilly task.
They scoop the snow from either side
And bandage up the poorly slide.
Tread on it, trample it, smooth it, thump it.
'If that don't work, we'll have to jump it!'
'Jump what?' says Denis, looking queasy.
'The gap!' says Alice. 'Easy-peasy!'

Elsewhere in the playground, the usual scene:
A teacher on duty, it's Mrs Green.
A huddle of (mostly) shivering mums;
Some wondering babies, sucking thumbs
(Watching the world from way behind
As they wait in a queue of a different kind).
A gang of girls, they're shivering, too,
Discussing who'll be friends with who.
A little infant darting about,
Giving his birthday invites out.
While scattered here and there besides,
Half a dozen smaller slides.
Snowball battles, snowball chases,
Swimming kit and violin cases:
A student with a tiger skin,
And *fourteen* children to carry it in.

The slide, meanwhile, with its cold compress,
Restored to health, well, more or less,
Remains by far the star attraction,
As Denis and Co. glide back into action.
With breath like smoke and cheeks like roses,
Pounding hearts and runny noses,
Eyes a-sparkle, nerves a-quiver,
Not a chance of a chill or a sign of a shiver
(It's a funny thought, that – it's nice – it's neat:
A thing made of ice and it generates heat),
They slide and queue and slide again;
There's six in a line – no, seven – no, ten!

A motley crew, a happy band,
Attending their own strip of land.
'Fifty foot long by two foot wide!'
'By half an inch thick!' – that's the mighty slide.
Cool and grey and, now, complete.
A work of art, all done by feet.

Then, suddenly, a whistle blows,
And all the human dynamos
(With outstretched arms and just-bent knees)
Skid to a halt, fall silent, freeze.
They stand in a trance, their hot breath steaming;
Rub their eyes as though they've been dreaming,
Or are caught in the bossy whistle's spell,
Or simply weary – it's hard to tell.
A few of them shiver, the air feels cool;
And the thought sinks in: it's time for school.

A little while later, observe the scene,
Transformed by a whistle and Mrs Green:
The empty playground, white and wide;
The scruffy snow, the silent slide.

Inside, with a maths card just begun
And his thoughts elsewhere, sits Denis Dunne.
His hands are chapped, his socks are wet,
But in his head he's sliding yet.
He sits near a window, he stares through the glass.
The teacher frowns from the front of the class.
Can this boy move! Can this boy skate!
'Come on, Denis – concentrate!'
Yes, nothing changes, that much is true,
And the chances of sliding in classrooms are few.
So Denis abandons his speculation,
And gets on with his education.

Some plough the land, some mow or mine it;
While others – if you let them – shine it.

Captain Jim

You've heard the tales of Tarzan,
Chinese Charlie Chan,
Sherlock Holmes of Baker Street
And 'cow pie' Desperate Dan;
Well, now I'm going to tell you
Of another kind of man.

Yes, now I'm going to tell you,
As the light grows dim,
And we sit here in the jungle
At the wide world's rim,
Of the man who matched them all:
And his name was Captain Jim.

Where he came from is a mystery,
Where he went to no one knows,
But his talents were amazing
(From his eyebrows to his toes!),
And his brain was full of brainwaves,
And his reputation grows.

It all began one summer
Near this very spot,
When the river-boats were steaming
And the river banks were hot,
And the *crocodiles* were teeming,
Which sometimes a child forgot.

I was playing with my brothers,
Bertie, Joe and little Frank,
In the mangrove trees that twisted
From that mossed and muddy bank;
When young Frank climbed out too far,
Slipped and fell, and straightways – sank.

Hardly had he hit the water,
Barely had the ripples spread,
When the river started foaming
And we saw with awful dread
Half a dozen snapping snouts
In a hurry to be fed.

Well, we shouted and we threw things,
Lumps of rock and bits of wood,
And young Frank, he cried for help
And tried to swim as best he could,
But the crocs were closing in
And it wasn't any good.

Then at last when all seemed lost,
And it was looking grim,
There was a *blur* beside us,
And a man leapt in to swim
Like an arrow from a bow:
And his name was Captain Jim.

He was dressed, we later noticed,
In a suit of gleaming white,
And he even had his hat on;
Oh, it was a stirring sight,
As he surged into the fray
Like a charge of dynamite.

With his bare hands and a cricket bat,
He gave the crocs what for;
Hit the six of them for six,
Though I doubt they kept the score.
Then he gave a tow to little Frank
And calmly swam to shore.

And that was the beginning,
The first time he was seen,
In the heat and haze of summer
When the air itself was green
And the river banks were steaming ...
And he chose to intervene.

Where he came from is a mystery,
Why he stayed we never knew,
But he took a room at Macey's
And he moored his own canoe
At the wharf beside the warehouse.
And he bought a cockatoo.

Now this, I should remind you,
Was twenty years ago,
In nineteen thirty-one,
When the pace of life was slow,
And Grandpa ran the Copper Mine
And built this bungalow.

And the town was smaller then,
Just some houses and a pier,
And the Steamship Company Office
With a barber's at the rear,
And a visiting policeman
Who came by four times a year.

So it took no time at all
For the tale to get about;
How the stranger with a cricket bat
Had fished young Frankie out,
And hammered *fourteen* crocodiles
With one enormous clout.

And as the weeks went by,
There were other tales to tell:
How he saved the Baxters' baby
(With the speed of a gazelle!)
And the Baxters' baby's teddy –
It was needing help as well.

How he stopped a charging wart hog
As it rampaged through the town
(Knocking bikes and fences flying,
Pulling wires and washing down),
With a matadorial flourish
And a matadorial frown.

Well, we followed him about, of course,
Or watched him where he sat
On Macey's back verandah
In his dazzling suit and hat,
With a glass of tea beside him,
And – sometimes – Macey's cat.

We listened to the gossip
Inside the barber's shop.
Some said he was a gambler,
Some said he was a cop,
And oaths were sworn and bets were laid
On just how long he'd stop.

We eavesdropped on the talk
Outside the General Store.
They marvelled at his manicure
And at the clothes he wore.
Whoever did his laundry?
What was that cricket bat *for*?

In time the summer ended;
The rains began to fall;
Moss clung to the houses
And creepers covered all.
The river was a torrent
And the grass grew eight feet tall.

And still he lived among us
And continued to amaze,
With his quick, explosive actions,
And his steady *brainy* gaze;
Though he gave no thought to wages,
And he never looked for praise.

And he showed us how to wrestle,
And he taught us how to dive,
And he saved us from the wild bees –
We had blundered on a hive –
When he walloped it to safety
With a perfect cover drive.

He delivered Mrs Foster's fourth,
When Doc Gains fell down drunk.
(The doctor diagnosed himself:
'I'm drunker than a skunk!')
Then Captain Jim took care of *him*,
And tucked him in his bunk.

At Christmas, when a touring troupe
Arrived to do a show,
And the tenor caught a fever
And it was touch-and-go,
Who was it calmly took his place?
Well, I expect you know.

And so the seasons passed,
And the months became a year,
And he saved us from a cheetah,
And he bought us ginger beer,
And he taught us how to make our own ...
And when to interfere.

He said: the world's a puzzle,
A game of keys and locks;
A mirror in a mirror,
A box within a box;
And we must do the best we can
And stand up to the shocks.

He told us: that's the moral,
In a world without a plan,
In a world without a meaning,
Designed to puzzle man;
You must do your intervening
In the best way that you can.

Some said he was a writer,
And some, a diplomat;
A traveller, spy, geologist,
And various things like that.
We said he was a cricketer;
How else explain the bat?

'You'd been on tour,' said little Frank.
'And scored a ton,' said Joe.
'And when the boat returned to home,'
Said I, 'you didn't go.'
But when we asked him was it true,
He said, 'Well . . . yes and no.'

And he built a bridge that summer,
And he made a mighty kite,
And he saved us from the axeman,
Who was 'axing' for a fight,
And he beat the Mayor at poker,
And he caught quail in the night.

He read the weeks-old papers,
And played the gramophone,
And climbed the hills above the town,
And watched the sky alone,
And taught the barber's daughter chess
(Who's now your Auntie Joan).

Then, one evening in September,
As we sat up on the pier,
With our mango-chutney sandwiches
And home-made ginger beer,
And our Steamboat Billy comics ...
We saw him disappear.

In his suit of gleaming white
And his loaded-up canoe,
He passed quickly out of sight,
There was nothing we could do.
He had paid his bill at Macey's;
And he took the cockatoo.

Well, we shouted from the quayside
And we ran along the bank,
And scrambled in the mangroves,
Delayed by little Frank;
But he was gone for evermore,
And left behind ... a blank.

Yet not quite a blank, perhaps,
For he did leave us a note
And some marbles (c/o Macey's),
And this is what he wrote:
'Watch out for life's crocodiles,
And try to stay afloat.'

Why he came remained a mystery,
Why he left us, no one knows,
But his talents were amazing
(From his eyebrows to his toes!),
And though it's now all history,
Still his reputation grows:

The voice of Nelson Eddy,
The dash of Errol Flynn,
The brains of Albert Einstein,
The speed of Rin Tin Tin,
The cover drive of Bradman,
The pluck of Gunga Din.

That's how we have remembered,
As the years grow dim
And life slips slowly by
On the wide world's rim,
The man who matched them all:
And his name was Captain Jim.

Now little Frank is bigger,
And Bertie's married Joan,
And Joe's become an engineer
With 'Wireless-Telephone',
And I tell bedtime stories
To children of my own.

One final thing, before I go
(I heard your mother call);
A few years back, it must have been,
When you were both quite small,
I bought some cigarette cards
At the Monday Market Stall.

Woodbine's Famous Cricketers,
Fifty in the set;
They were faded, creased and dog-eared,
Badly stained with dust and sweat;
Yet there was a face among them
That I never could forget.

It was him all right, I'd swear it;
It was him without a doubt,
With his bat raised in a flourish
Letting go a mighty clout.
'Captain James Fitz . . . (blur),' it stated:
'Four-forty-nine not out.'

The Girl who Doubled

This is the story
Of Alison Hubble,
Who went to bed single
And woke up double.

Woke up with a twin
In her single bed.
'Who are you?' 'Who are *you*?'
She said, she said.

Then her dad came in.

'Good grief! Ye gods!'
Mr Hubble declared,
As he gazed at the sight
Of Alison squared.

'I can't believe it;
It's hardly fair;
One daughter's enough,
We don't need a pair!'

Then Mrs Hubble came in.

'Oh Alison, *Alison!*'
Cried her mother.
'You always said you wanted a *brother*.

'I'm quite overcome.
Your gran'll go wild.
We don't expect this
From an only child.'

Later on, the doctor was sent for.

'Hmm!' said the doctor.
'What have we here?
Whatever it is,
It's double, I fear.

'If you've had it before,
Well, you've got it again.'
Then he felt in his pocket
And took out a pen,
And wrote a prescription
(But gave no advice),
Just some pills to be taken,
Twice daily – twice.

After he'd gone, Alison had a word (or two).

'I want to get up!'
'That goes for me!'
'I'm hungry and thirsty!'
'And *bored*!' 'I agree!'

So up she got
And washed her faces
(Leaving soap in the usual places).

Then: what to wear?
'Yes, that's the trouble;
I'm in two minds,' said Alison Hubble.

By and by Alison went to school, with a letter
for the teacher.

Dear Mrs Mott (it said),
I thought I ought to write
A note about our Alison
Who doubled in the night.
Her father and I
Were powerless to prevent
What can only be described
As this singular event.
We're sorry indeed
To put you to this trouble,
Yours sincerely, Maureen Hubble.

P.S. Her extra dinner money is enclosed.

Well, at first it was fun –
Lots of laughs;
And a queue formed at play time
For her autographs.

She played hide-and-seek;
She skipped with her friends,
Did the 'double whip'
And held both ends.

Presently, however, there was a spot of bother.

Her friends said, 'But Alison,
Which one's really you?
Come on, we're flummoxed;
Give us a clue!'

'Well, *I'm* me,' said Alison.
And, 'I'm me, too!'
'No you're not – what rubbish!'
'I'm more me than you!'

Then Alison gave herself a shove,
And another in reply;
And called herself names,
And made herself cry.

She turned to her pals
With the usual plea:
'Don't be friends with her –
Be friends with me!'

Later, in the cloakroom, while the girls were
getting changed for games, something else happened.

The cloakroom was crowded,
But got crowded even more,
When – all of a sudden –
There was Alison times four!

She had doubled again,
In seconds flat;
Like magical rabbits
From a conjuror's hat.

Her friends were delighted
And concerned for her fate.
'Poor Alison!' they sympathized.
And, 'This is great!'

They argued in the hockey match
Which team she should be in.
'With Alison in goal,
We'd be bound to win!'

Then it was home time.

When Alison came through the door
And kept on coming,
Her father put his glasses on
And starting drumming
With his fingers on the table;
And then he said, 'Ye gods!
It was bad enough before.
Now we've got quads!'

'That's true,' said her mother;
'I quite agree.
She's doing it on purpose,
If you ask me.

'Is this all the thanks we get?
Do something, Ted!
Whatever will the neighbours say?'
Mrs Hubble said.

'They'll put two and two together;
Still, they'll hardly say,'
Said Mr Hubble glumly,
'That she's wasting away.'

Alison, for her part, defended herselves.

'It's not *my* fault,' she said.
'Don't blame me!'
'Blame her!' 'And her!' simultaneously.

Then she went outside,
And upstairs, too;
And sat in the kitchen,
And sat on the loo;

Did the washing up
And some of the drying,
Ran into the garden
And knocked herself flying.

As he watched his daughter
Coming and going,
Eating and drinking, catching and throwing,
Mr Hubble announced,
'I feel quite dizzy.
However can one child *be* so busy?'

Soon the phone started ringing,
And the doorbell, too;
It was Alison's friends,
Give or take a few
Who were friends of friends
Or friends' younger brothers:
Could Alison come out to play,
And could she bring ... the others?

So Alison played for a while until tea time.

Then: 'Cheese for me!' she said.
'I'd like ham!'
'Boiled egg and salad, please!'
'Bread and jam!'

And Mrs Hubble muttered
While she did her best,
'I've somehow got the feeling
We've a cuckoo in the nest.'

At nine o'clock Alison went to bed.

Two of her slept in the spare room,
And two in her usual bed.
Two had a bedtime story;
Two read to herself instead.

She tip-toed on the landing,
Giving herself a scare,
As she whispered in the darkness:
'Alison, you still there?'

And before she went to sleep,
Each one of her stared at the ceiling,
With a puzzled look on her face
And a curious *quadruple* feeling.

When morning came, Mrs Hubble
Called to her husband, 'Ted!
Wake up, come on, go and count her.
I can't bear to look,' she said.

So Alison's father arose
And peered anxiously in at each door.
'There's two in here,' he reported;
'And two in here makes four.'

'And two downstairs!' cried Alison.
'And two in the bath makes ten!'
(Maths wasn't her strongest subject.)
'I think I've doubled again!'

Later, she had her breakfasts and her friends
called for her.

Then, off to school went Alison (cloned),
Wearing most of the clothes
She had ever owned.

Well, a crowd was waiting
At the playground gate
With a noisy welcome:
'Two – four – six – eight!'

A reporter was there
From the local press.
'Who's Alison Hubble?'
And the crowd said, 'Guess!'

The photographer with him
Lined Alison up
Like a football team
That had won the cup.

Eventually, Alison reached her classroom.

'Alison Hubble?' 'Here, Miss!'
'Here, Miss!' 'Here, Miss!' 'Hey!
Hang on there, whoa!' said Mrs Mott.
'We'll be here all day.'

Extra books were sent for;
Extra chairs and tables.
Said Mrs Mott (all muddled up),
'What you girls need is labels!'

Meanwhile, the news was spreading,
And not too far away
Graffiti in the High Street
Said: ALISON RULES OK

When school ended, Alison came home to find
her dad in his best suit.

And her mum, looking brave
With a cup of tea,
Being interviewed for the BBC
While the crowd in the street
Went, 'Oooh!' and 'Aaah!'
'Here's Alison et cetera.'
There were TV cameras,
A TV van,
Microphones, cables, and Alison's gran,

Who was complaining about the injustice of it all.

'I can't understand it,
She's not a barbarian.
She goes to *church* –
She's a Unitarian!'

And Alison, too,
Had complaints of her own.
'I'm fed up with crowds;
I want to be alone!'

She refused to be filmed
For the News at Ten,
Stamped up to her room ...
And doubled again.

'Oh, no!' said her mum.
'What a tragedy!
It'll take us two hours
To cook her tea.'

'You're right,' said her dad.
'It's rotten luck.
We'll have to do the shopping
With a three-ton truck.'

Alison herself, however, cheered up when
she saw the *tent* in the back garden.

Yes, out on the lawn
Stood a large bell tent
With sleeping bags, too,
Which the Council had lent.

'Is that for me,
Or should I say us?'
And she let out a yell that was thunderous.

Yet even then
There were certain snags,
When she doubled that night
And got stuck in the bags.

In case you've lost count, there were now
thirty-two of her.

Well, Alison's fame
Continued to spread.
'SHE'S ONE IN A MILLION',
The papers said.

Mrs Thatcher dropped in
And (huskily) told her:
'We *do* hope you'll vote for us,
When you're older.'

While a man in the dock,
In serious trouble,
Said: 'Not me, m'lud –
It was Alison Hubble!'

Various professors and experts also took an
interest in her.

They studied her tongues
And tapped her knees
And talked of split personalities.

'It's something in the water!'
'Something she ate!'
'An act of God!'
'The Russians!' 'Fate!'

And they wondered
Where the world was heading,
And whether or not
They could stop her spreading.

Well, they're wondering yet,
If you care to know,
For the numbers of Alison
Continue to grow.

She's lately reached
A huge amount,
Though how many's uncertain;
They've all lost count.

Meanwhile, the government is getting worried.

'If she multiplies
At her present rate,
We'll be shoved off the Earth
By 2008!
Yes, the Universe
Reduced to rubble,
Just on account of Alison Hubble.'

Meanwhile *Alison* ...

Who has, so to speak,
Grown out of her tent,
Is presently living
In Stoke-on-Trent.

All of it!

The History of

A Pair of Sinners

forgetting not their Ma
who was one also

1. *Wherein the Harrises and their Dishonest*
Trade are Introduced

In London Town some years ago
There dwelt a pair of sinners.
His name was Jack, her name was Belle
And they was baby-skinners.

They was brother and sister too
I should perhaps just add;
Lived with their Ma above the shop;
They hadn't got no dad.

Now baby-skinning, though a crime,
Weren't quite so bad as you'd suppose.
A skinner never hurt a child,
He only skinned him of his clothes.

Jack and Belle would work like this:
First, spy a posh new pram,
Distract the nursemaid from her task,
Then grab the child and scram.

Or else they'd lure some toddler
For him to roam and stray,
Then do him up inside Jack's coat
And smuggle him away.

One time they had a horse and cart
And, with a criminal lad,
They pinched a little schoolful;
The mistress weren't half mad.

Well, having got a child, y'see,
They'd skin him swift and neat,
Then leave him in his cotton drawers
A-shivering in the street.

Skinners, according to the police,
Most thrived when summer was gone.
The streets was gloomier places then,
And a child had more clothes on.

The shop which Mrs Harris kept,
That was their mother's name,
Sold baby clothes – I 'spect you guessed.
She was a crafty dame.

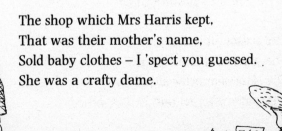

She washed 'n' ironed 'n' dyed the things
All colours under the sun.
She altered them with ribbons and such,
My word, she did have fun.

Then in the window they would go
Or on a tailor's rack.
Sometimes the folks they'd pinched things off
Come in and bought 'em back.

So, there y'are, that's Jack and Belle
And their dishonest trade.
And their dishonest mother too,
With a fortune being made.

Still, crime don't hardly ever pay;
Justice will lie in wait;
And how the Harrises met their end,
I'll now to you relate.

II. *Wherein the Particulars of a Bad Business
in St James's Park are Given*

The season, it is winter;
The place, St James's Park;
The time, a quarter after four,
Just starting to get dark.

A nursemaid and her little charge
Are playing with a sledge.
They do not spot Jack Harris
A-crouched behind the hedge.

Now Belle gets talking to the maid
And asking her the way;
And while she points directions out
Her charge remains at play.

The child shouts, 'Whee!' as down he slides
Across the gleaming snow.
Until, that is, Jack grabs him,
And then he hollers, 'Oh!'

When she observes the empty sledge
And the fleeing figure of Jack,
The nursemaid says, 'That's torn it,
I 'spect I'll get the sack!'

Then with a start she recollects
Instructions she has had,
And takes a whistle from her bag
And blows the thing like mad.

Meanwhile, of course, the Harrises,
Having seen their plan succeed,
Are scooting off by different routes
To a place they have agreed.

Jack, for his part, is puffing hard
With the load he has to tote.
It ain't such easy work to run
With a infant up y'coat.

Nor it ain't so easy neither
Knowing best what course to steer
When the keepers of the park approach
And the constables appear.

But the police, at least, is busy
Taking statements from the maid
And pondering Jack's footprints
In the snow where they was laid.

The rendez-vous is a shrubbery
Just in St James's Square.
When Jack arrives, exhausted like,
He finds Belle waiting there.

'Oh, Jack,' says Belle, as she regards
The luckless, pilfered child,
'We've got a little gold-mine here.
Look how his coat is styled!

'Look at his shirt and his little hat.
Look at this glove – it's kid!
And here, these boots – what beauties,
They must be worth a quid!'

The child, I'm happy to report,
Don't seem too much offended,
But stands a-sucking of his thumb
And hears hisself commended.

Jack, though, is worried, that is plain.
'Y'see,' he says to Belle,
'There is some funny business here;
I know it – I can tell.

'A whistle, well, that ain't so strange,
Nor coppers, come to that.
But when y'gets the Coldstream Guards
It's time to smell a rat!'

Jack was right – the guards was out,
And the Horse Artillery too.
The streets was teeming full of police,
It was a real to-do,

With shouts and lanterns in the square,
The tumult of trotting hoofs;
And watchmen searching houses,
Even climbing on the roofs.

Yet Belle keeps up her interest
In the child's sartorial charms,
Until upon his vest she spies
A certain coat-of-arms.

She spies it on his socks likewise.
Then in a voice of dread,
She says, 'Is your name ... Bertie?'
The child, he nods his head.

'God bless my heart,' says Belle.
Her rosy cheek it pales.
'I think I know what's happened, Jack.
We've pinched the Prince of Wales!'

Which was the truth and did explain
The mighty hue and cry.
For there was halberdiers passing now,
And cannon rolling by.

'Well, knock me down with a feather,' says Jack.
'What a horrible, rotten trick.
Who ever would have thought it?
Here – get his clothes on quick!'

So Jack and Belle re-dress the Prince
And give his shoes a shine.
They're clumsy, as y'might expect:
Un-dressing's more their line.

Belle strikes a match to scrutinize
The small unflappable lad.
'He's tidier now than he was with his nurse,'
She says. 'That can't be bad.'

'What bothers me,' Jack Harris says,
'Is what to tell our mother.
I mean, see, skinning's one thing –
High treason, that's another.'

'Oh, don't say that,' Belle whispers.
'He'll get the wrong idea.'
She drops a curtsy to the Prince.
'Can I, er ... speak to you, m'dear?

'Look here, y'little majesty,
This is a false alarm.
We are your loyalest subjects.
We never meant no harm.'

'No, just a joke,' says Jack,
'That's all what was intended.
You better toddle home now.
Your ma might be offended.'

But Belle, from being truly loyal,
Won't hear of such a thing.
They cannot very well desert
The country's future king.

Besides, the Prince is disinclined
To leave the shrubbery.
It makes him think of Robin Hood,
And, 'I want to play,' says he.

Then for his sword he seizes up
A hefty piece of wood,
And waves it vigorously on high
Just like a outlaw should.

Thus, for a time, unwillingly,
The Harrises are stuck
With Belle in the role of Marian
And Jack as Friar Tuck.

While the little Prince in wild delight
Goes charging here and there,
A-bossing of his men about
And saving his lady fair.

'Be careful with y'sword, my liege,'
Says Belle, provoked to speak.
'You bang my brother's head like that,
He'll be in bed for a week!'

'Not only – aargh! – that,' shouts Jack,
As he suffers a clout again.
'Why fight with me at all?
I'm one of his Merrie – aargh! – Men.'

Belle says, 'Hush up there, do;
You'll give us all away.'
'Hush up y'self,' Jack mutters.
'It's me he's trying to slay.'

Presently the Prince gets fagged
From all the rogues he's smote,
And says it is his wish to ride
Inside Jack Harris's coat.

I expect this was a novel thing
For so well-raised a lad.
It's doubtful if he got the chance
When he was with his dad.

Though sulking yet from previous hurts
And mindful of further blows,
Jack buttons up the royal boy
Till not a hair of him shows.

By now, of course, it is quite dark.
Snow has begun to fall.
The weary Prince is dozing off.
Belle covers her head with a shawl.

'Let's risk it and smuggle him back,' says she.
'Just up to the palace gate.'
She clutches her shawl. 'Be a patriot, Jack!
Come on, it's getting late.'

Jack weighs this up for a minute.
He has a look in the square.
The snow is thick and swirling.
There hardly seems nobody there.

'Right-o,' says he. 'I ever was
A tender-hearted man.'
He takes Belle's arm; they ventures forth.
'Look nonchalant, if y'can.'

Out from the square the Harrises trot
Into a narrow street.
They hear the cry of a bellman;
The tramp of muffled feet.

A coster-lady calls to them
From the steps of a hotel.
'Bad business this, about the Prince!'
'Oh, terrible,' says Belle.

A chimney-sweeper hurries by;
The snow piled on his hat.
'You've heard the news?' 'We have,' says Jack.
'Who'd do a thing like that?'

At last they come into the Mall.
The Prince is still a-snoozing.
'We're winning, Jack,' his sister says.
Then, lo and behold, they're losing.

The snow, it suddenly abates.
A street lamp lights the scene.
A chilly fear invests Belle's heart
Where her warm hopes had been.

Now up the Mall a carriage drives,
Its springs and harness jigging.
Inside, the nursemaid looking peeved;
The Queen has give her a wigging,

And sent her off to join the search.
The maid stares mournfully out;
Claps eyes on the approaching Jack
And gives a grateful shout.

'That's him – look, there – and her likewise!'
The carriage skids to a halt.
Whistles and bugles rend the air.
Says Belle, 'It's all my fault.'

Meanwhile, the little sleeping Prince,
Roused by the hullabaloo,
Protrudes his head out of Jack's coat
Like the son of a kangaroo.

'Pity we never brought his sword,'
Says Jack, by way of a quip.
'He could've smacked a few of their heads
While you and me give 'em the slip.'

For Jack well knows the jig is up.
No man should hope to flee;
Not when he's getting cornered
By the Household Cavalry.

Soon from the park a mighty horde
Of constables appear,
And boldly cry, 'Hallo, hallo,
Now then, what's going on here?'

'I doubt if you'll believe this, sirs,'
Says the perspiring Jack;
'But this child was took erroneously.
We was just bringing him back.'

'A likely tale, my shifty lad,'
The officers reply.
'You'll tell us next you're Robin Hood.'
'Oh, no,' says Jack. 'Not I.'

III. *Wherein the Scene of this History is Closed*

The trial of all the Harrises
(Their Ma got nabbed as well)
Took place at the Old Bailey
As I shall briefly tell.

To avoid the charge of treason,
What they found they had to do
Was own up to their actual crime
And more or less prove it too.

Thus, a crowd of little infants
Was called and took the oath,
Swore Jack and Belle had skinned 'em
And recognized them both.

The nursemaid gave her evidence,
And the sledge – Exhibit A –
Was held aloft in the courtroom
For the jury to survey.

The royal Prince did not appear.
He had been sent to bed
For applying his father's walking-stick
To a elderly footman's head.

'But you also claim it was a joke,'
Said the judge to the accused.
'Well, I'll tell you this for nothing,
The Queen was not amused.'

Then he sentenced them to go to jail
For a couple of years apiece,
And hoped that when they was let out
Their criminal ways would cease.

And cease they did, it can be said,
For now the Harrises keep
A pet shop in the Brompton Road:
BEST DOGS AND BUDGIES – CHEEP!

Postscript

Unfortunately, I have just heard,
While the above was being wrote,
Jack was seen leaving London Zoo
With a parrot up his coat.

Belle Harris had distracted
The keeper and his men.
I fear the pair of 'em has gone back
To sinning once again.

Historical Note

Child Stripping – This is generally done by females, old debauched drunken hags who watch their opportunity to accost children passing in the streets, tidily dressed with good boots and clothes. They entice them away to a low or quiet neighbourhood for the purpose, as they say, of buying them sweets, or with some other pretext. When they get into a convenient place, they give them a halfpenny or some sweets, and take off the articles of dress, and tell them to remain till they return, when they go away with the booty.

This is done most frequently in mews in the West-end, and at Clerkenwell, Westminster, the Borough, and other similar localities. These heartless debased women sometimes commit these felonies in the disreputable neighbourhoods where they live, but more frequently in distant places, where they are not known and cannot be easily traced. This mode of felony is not so prevalent in the metropolis as formerly. In most cases, it is done at dusk in the winter evenings, from 7 to 10 o'clock.

From Henry Mayhew's
London Labour and the London Poor,
Vol. IV (published 1862)

The Scariest Yet

There was rain at the windows
And wind in the yard,
And the clock said a quarter past three.
The children complained
That their work was too hard,
And the teacher said, 'Right – I agree!'

Then, quick as a blink,
The books disappeared
And desk-lids machine-gunned the air.
The children sat smiling,
A few of them cheered
And the teacher leant back in his chair.

'Tell us a story!' the children said,
'Like The Tale of the Two-Headed Man,
Or The Mad Professor's Daughter,
Or The Terror of Turkestan.
Tell us a story like Marley's Ghost,
Or The Ruffian on the Stairs,
Or The Girl who got Boiled in a Barrel of Oil,
Or The Boy who got Eaten by Bears!'

There was fish in the fish-tank
And chalk on the board
And waste in the waste-paper bin;
And joy in the hearts
Of the Class Six horde
When the teacher said, 'Right – I'll begin!'

This story is one I've not told before;
I think I might call it The Boiler-Room Door,
Or The Beast from Below, or Stan in a Sweat;
But one thing's for sure – it's the scariest yet!
(*The children, meanwhile, settled back in their places,*
An 'Oooh!' on their lips, a flush on their faces.)
And it all began in the Second World War,
February, nineteen forty-four;
In a school much like ours, with kids much like you;
And it's horribly strange, and it's utterly true.

Well, really those were the bad old days
When we were deprived in a hundred ways.
Sweets were rationed, bananas rare;
You couldn't get oranges anywhere.
Chicken and cheese were in short supply;
We made do with whalemeat and rabbit pie.
You fancied ice-cream? Y'hopes were slight;
There were queues in the morning and bombs at night.
And I think you lot would've gone demented;
Fish-fingers hadn't been invented!

So, there you are, just a few ideas
Of what it was like in those earlier years:
The rations, the queues, the bombs, the war;
And on top of all that, there was something more ...

One night a boy named Stanley Fox
Pulled down his cap and up his socks,
Kissed his mother and cuddled the cat,
Drank his Oxo in seconds flat,
Grabbed his torch and his threepenny subs,
And hurried off to the Rolfe Street cubs.

The streets were dark, though the moon was out,
And Stanley didn't hang about.
He called for his best friend, Sidney Poole,
And together they raced to Rolfe Street School.
Sidney was plump, with his arm in a sling
(From fooling around on his sister's swing).
Stanley was older and taller and thinner,
Which was hard to believe when you saw his dinner.
They had been best friends since the war began,
And were generally known as Sid 'n' Stan.

As they shone their way down the blacked-out street,
Other beams converged to meet
In the gap that was once the old school gate
(Now melted down for armoured plate).
Other voices, other boys;
Shouts and shoving; laughter – noise!
Then through the gap or over the wall
They jostled and whooped in the infants' hall.

Then followed the usual 'dibs and dubs',
The singing of songs, the paying of subs,
The tying of knots, the reading of maps,
The jokes about Germans, the jokes about Japs.
Towards the end, Akela said,
'We'll have a few games, then home to bed!'
So they played British Bulldog and Pig in the Ring,
All except Sid on account of his sling;
And hide-and-seek – they scattered and hid;
Akela joined in, and so did Sid.
From force of habit he followed Stan.
It was just about then . . . that the trouble began.

'Five – ten – fifteen – twenty!'
The places to hide in that school were plenty.
It was old – like ours – well, older really.
(*'Older 'n you, Sir?' 'Yes – well, nearly.'*)
But Sidney and Stanley were trouble bound,
For the place to avoid was the place they found.
Not the cloakrooms, the stage or the P.E. store,
But the steps leading down to the boiler-room door.

The boiler-room was below the school;
The caretaker kept it locked as a rule.
However, this particular night,
When nothing for Sid 'n' Stan went right,
The door was ajar – 'What a place to hide!' –
And with hardly a thought they went inside,
Confident no one ever would find them,
And shut the heavy door behind them.

'Ninety-five – a hundred – coming-ready-or-not!'
It was pitch-dark in the boiler-room, dusty and hot.
'You there?' said Stan. 'I can't see a thing!'
'Nor me,' said Sid; then: 'Mind me sling!'
'More steps, I think,' Stan said. 'Watch out!'
Then he lost his footing and gave a shout.
Sid fumbled his way and followed the sound,
Till he fell over Stan where he lay on the ground.
'Damn it!' said Stan. 'Sod it!' said Sid.
'You thought of this!' 'I never!' 'Y'did!'
Sid rubbed his knee; Stan rubbed his head.
'I think I've cracked me skull,' he said.

Then – slowly – still rubbing the painful bits,
Sidney and Stanley recovered their wits.
As their eyes grew accustomed to the dark,
They could see the glow (and occasional spark)
From the flickering flame at the furnace door,
And vague shapes, too, on the boiler-room floor.
Some boxes, perhaps, and a window pole;
A pile of, maybe, coke or coal;
A sack of something – a bucket – a mop;
A table with a chair on top.

Meanwhile, in the corridor, clattering feet
And echoing voices: 'Got y'Pete!'
Stan felt a sudden flutter of fear:
Whatever made us come down here?
The hair rose up on the back of his neck;
He turned his head, and – 'Bloody heck!'
Stan's throat felt strangled, his voice a croak,
As over the pile of coal or coke . . .
(He clutched Sid's arm, and caught his sling)
Came a huge and shapeless, lumbering thing!

Sid struggled to speak (he'd seen it, too),
But the best he could manage was, 'S-Stan!' and 'Oow!'
They jumped up then and tried to run,
Which, of course, was easier said than done.
They scrambled and staggered and stumbled and fell,
And what would've happened, it's hard to tell.
(For behind them 'whatever-it-was' was near;
Its appalling breathing plain to hear.)

Well, what *did* happen was, suddenly – bang!
The door flew open and Freddy Lang
Yelled down the steps, 'I see you, Sid!'
Then leapt aside – good job he did –
As out of that cellar came Sid 'n' Stan
Like shots from a gun or Superman.
They slammed the door, grabbed hold of Fred,
Said not a word, but turned – and fled.

There was steam on the windows
And sleet in the air,
And the clock said twenty to four.
The children protested
'Oh, Sir, it's not fair!'
'Don't stop now!' 'Y'can't!' 'Tell us more!'

'Yes, what happened next?' the children said.
'Did it get 'em and eat 'em up?'
'Did it crunch their bones in the blacked-out streets?'
'Did it drink their blood from a cup?'
'Was it Dracula, Sir, or Frankenstein –
This lumbering sort of creature?'
'The Hunchback of Notre-Dame, perhaps?
King Kong or – ' 'Got it – a teacher!'

And they said, 'Oh, Sir, you swore!
We're going to tell on you.'
'You said "bloody", we heard you, Sir;
And "damn it" and "sod it", too.'
While the teacher, putting his coat on,
Said, 'Swear – no, I never did.
It wasn't me – come on, home time!
Oh, no – it was Stan 'n' Sid.'

There was ice on the windows
The following day,
And the sky was frosty and pale.
Class Six settled quickly
From afternoon play,
And the teacher continued his tale.

So Stanley Fox and Sidney Poole
Got the shock of their lives at Rolfe Street School;
Put in a panic and scared half to death
By a shadowy shape and the sound of breath.

They told Akela, 'Its face was sort of hairy!'
They told the others, 'Its hands were sort of claws!'
They told their mothers, 'Its eyes were sort of starey!'
They told themselves, 'It crunched coke in its jaws!'
For already their memories embroidered the scene,
Mixing the truth with what-might've-been.
(This often occurs just after a fright;
Although, as it happens, this time they were right.)

However, Akela was meeting a friend,
And hurried the pair of them home in the end;
While their mothers more noticed the bruises and dirt:
'Just look at y'jumper!' 'Y'scamp – does it hurt?'
Thus bathed and bandaged, confused, relieved,
Unpursued but unbelieved,
They climbed the stairs to their separate beds,
And pulled the bedclothes over their heads.

When Stan woke up the following morning,
Eyes full of sleep, mouth full of yawning,
His curtains were open, the sun was high,
There wasn't a single cloud in the sky;
His clean clothes lay on his bedside chair
And a smell of breakfast filled the air.
In a world so golden and shining and clean,
It was hard to believe what he *thought* he'd seen;
Then he felt the bruise on the side of his head,
And shivered in his cosy bed.

When Sid came round at half-past eight,
Stan's mum declared, '*You're* in a state!
Arm in a sling and a bandaged knee;
You're worse than him, if you ask me.
Have you been seeing monsters, too?'
And Sid smiled weakly, 'Well – a few!'

As they left the house at twenty to nine,
Sid said, 'Your mum's as bad as mine.
Mine hardly believes a thing I tell her;
Especially monsters seen in a cellar.'
Stan nodded his head, he had to agree.
Then: 'I wasn't all *that* scared.' 'Nor me!'
'I'd go down again, if you bet me a quid.'
'I'd go for a couple of bob,' said Sid.
'Mind you, it was big – well, I think it was big.'
'And covered in hair, like a bloomin' great wig!'
And so they rehearsed a description to fit it.
And, of course, they *were* scared, but scared to admit it.

In the playground with the other kids
There was further talk of bets and quids.
For the news, as you might expect, had spread.
The rest of the cubs, especially Fred,
Had told the tale, or what was known,
And even added bits of their own.
'Look out, who's here?' 'It's Sid 'n' Stan!'
'They got chased by the Bogeyman!'
'King Kong, it was – or Doctor Death!'
'They seen his face!' 'They felt his breath!'
'It's true!' said Stan; 'We did!' said Sid.
'Bet you a tanner!' 'A dollar!' 'A quid!'
'Cross my heart and hope to die!'
'Monster, my foot!' 'Monster, my eye!'

At this point Sid had a worrying thought:
'We never warned old Mr Short!'
(He was the caretaker, first name Jim.)
'What if whatever-it-was gets him?'
'I shouldn't bother,' said Albert Crump.
'Old Jimmy Short'd make *him* jump.
Besides, I saw him shifting a bin
Just a minute ago, when I came in.'
'I seen him, too – it's true,' said Fred.
'He didn't look nice, but he didn't look dead.'

Later that morning, at half-past ten,
When the kids were back in the playground again,
Playing marbles, five-stones, tick,
Hopscotch with a bit of brick,
Swopping fag-cards, swopping punches,
Telling jokes and eating lunches,
Sid 'n' Stan just sat about,
Saying little and full of doubt.
The perfect health of Mr Short
Remained for them a disturbing thought.
A comfort, of course, but puzzling, too:
What *had* they seen? What should they *do*?

Just then a crowd went haring past,
With Fred at the front and Albert last.
Fred had a rope and an apple core.
'Hang on!' yelled Stan. 'What's all that for?'
'Brainwave!' cried Albert. 'Me and Fred –
We're going fishing – for monsters!' he said.
'We'll dangle the bait through the coal-chute grid.'
'You're barmy!' cried Stan. 'Wait for us!' shouted Sid.

Minutes later, the 'fishing' began,
Watched with mixed feelings by Sid 'n' Stan.
(Plus the owner of the skipping rope,
A second-year girl named Sophie Cope.)
Like Eskimos round a hole in the ice,
They eyed the line and offered advice.
'Give it a wiggle!' 'Give it a jerk!'
'My rope's getting dirty!' 'It's not gonna work!'
'Here, monster!' said Fred. 'Here, bogeyman!
I've got you a present from Sid 'n' Stan!'

Then, thinking to give the others a fright,
He pretended he'd actually got a bite;
Hauled on the line, 'A whopper!' he said.
Then – suddenly – scared himself instead.
For the bait had gone and the line was shorter.
A 'shark', it appeared, was patrolling the water.

The boys were amazed and appalled and thrilled.
Their flesh was crawling, their blood was chilled.
'It's ate the apple and – bloomin' hell –
It's ate the wooden 'andle as well!'
Yes, the boys were amazed, but the girl was mad:
'Me rope!' shouted Sophie. 'I'll tell our dad!'
While Sid looked at Stan and muttered, ' 'Strewth!'
I suppose after all we *was* telling the truth.'

There was fog at the windows,
Suspense in the room
And a class on the edge of its seat.
Their faces were white
In the gathering gloom,
And their hearts were missing a beat.

'And then *what happened?' the children cried.*
'Did it reach its paw through the grid?'
'Did it grab a hold of Albert Crump?'
'Did it take a lump out of Sid?'
'Could they hear it breathing down below?'
'Could they see its eyes in the dark?'
'What was that bit about Eskimos, Sir?'
'Did it really *bite like a shark?'*

There was noise from the corridor,
Noise from the hall
Where the fourth years were having P.E.
The teacher just smiled
And said nothing at all;
Only, 'Maybe,' and, 'Wait and see.'

Well, what happened next (he eventually said),
Was the whistle went and Albert and Fred
And Sophie and Sidney and Stanley and Co.
Trooped back into school for an hour or so,
To learn about fractions and Francis Drake,
Practise handwriting and bake a cake.
And talk about monsters and similar shocks
(A ghost in the youth club, a raid on the docks),
Talk in the toilets and under desk-lids,
Dare a few dares and bet a few quids,
Talk about Spitfires and Messerschmitts,
Relax their minds and recover their wits.

At dinner time it poured down with rain,
So they never did get in the playground again.
While home time was no time for hanging about;
When the school bell rang, the school was out.

Sidney and Stanley walked home up the street,
Discussing what a monster would eat.
'It crunches coke!' ('Our dog eats coal.')
'It swallows sacks of salvage whole!'
'It gets in the classrooms late at night,
And gives the guinea-pigs a bite!'
'Tulip bulbs!' 'Light bulbs!' 'Bean bags!' 'Yes –
Tadpoles and sticklebacks!' 'Mustard and cress!'
They stopped at a kerb and got splashed by a bus;
And Stanley said softly, 'It could've ate us.'

Half an hour later, at twenty-past four,
Stanley was eating and looking for more;
Till – hearing his friend at the backyard gate –
He grabbed his boots and, 'I won't be late!',
Bolted a biscuit and left like a shot
For the Thursday night match against Littlewood's lot.

This game was played in Victoria Park
From half-past four till when it got dark;
Eighteen a side and two half-times,
With a ball provided by Timothy Simes;
Coats for goals, one corner flag a tree,
A brook for a touch-line and *no* referee.
And Stan was left back and Sid on the wing,
Though he'd no business playing with his arm in a sling.

When the score was thirty : twenty-eight,
And the sky the colour of a classroom slate,
The teams all smothered in mud and sweat,
Steaming like horses and soaking wet,
And a boy named Horace had broken his glasses,
And *none* of them could see to make their passes,
They decided at last to call it a day,
And began to think what their mothers would say:
'What time d'you call this?' 'Get that mud off the floor!'
(Their fathers, of course, were away at the war.)

Through the darkened park with torches gleaming,
Painful knees and shirts still steaming,
Sid 'n' Stan with Albert and Fred
Replayed the match with their mouths instead.
'Did y'see that shot?' 'Did y'see that dive?'
'I scored a hat-trick!' 'I scored five!'
'We should've had a penalty!' 'Should've had three!'
'We'll hammer 'em next time – wait and see!'
They talked at length of the other team's failings,
And left the park through a gap in the palings.

'But what about the monster?' protested the class.
'This isn't a football story!'
'We don't want to hear about mothers and mud;
When is it going to get gory?'
The teacher was quiet for quite some time;
A small frown furrowed his brow.
'When is it going to get gory?' he said.
'Well, come to think of it ... now!'

The trouble really started with Timothy Simes:
'I've been in that boiler-room loads of times!'
'You never!' said Stan. 'You liar!' said Sid.
'Bet you a tanner!' 'A dollar!' 'A quid!'
They had bumped into Timmy in Mercer Street,
Having stopped at the fish shop for something to eat.
'Two penn'orth of chips!' 'A bag of batters, please!'
'A couple of scallops and a portion of peas!'

Well, a row had erupted while they were there,
Concerning the monster, its diet, its lair.
'I heard he swallowed a cricket bat.'
'No, an apple,' said Fred. 'Well, *I'd* eat that!
You're pulling my leg, you're having me on,
You never seen nothin' – it's all a big con!
I've been in that boiler-room loads of times;
It's bare as a barracks,' said Timothy Simes.
'We saw it,' said Stan. 'Well, prove it,' said Tim.
'I dare you – let's drop a few chips down on *'im*!'

And so it was at half-past seven
Under a black and starry heaven,
When they could've been home by a cosy fire
With toes thawing out and hair getting drier,
A mug of tea and the 'Radio Fun',
And nothing to fear from anyone,
Sidney and Stanley, breathing hard,
Found themselves in the Rolfe Street yard,
Picking their way over puddled ground,
Once more in a sweat, once more trouble bound.
And Albert and Freddy and Timmy were there,
And Timmy's friend, Denis, to witness the dare.

Six shadowy figures, five flickering beams
(The one without was Denis Eames),
Moving more slowly, fearing the worst;
Each trying to let the others go first.
When, all of a sudden, out of the night
Came a whistle of wind and a flash of light,
And a noise like the thump of a monstrous drum
As the school was blown to kingdom come;
Blitzed to bits – and dust – and rubble:
And that was only the start of the trouble.

The boys were lifted off their feet,
Their eyebrows singed in the searing heat.
Their clothes were torn, their chips were scattered
(And fried again, not that that mattered).
The mud on their boots and knees baked hard,
As they lay in a heap at the side of the yard;
Deafened and dazzled, bruised and grazed,
While the brickwork tumbled and the woodwork blazed.

The bomb, which had come as a total surprise
Out of the seemingly peaceful skies,
(No searchlights, no sirens) was hard to explain,
Though Fred later fancied he *had* heard a plane.
But, whatever the reasons, the likelihood
Was Rolfe Street had broken up for good.

Yes, the school was demolished, the landscape scarred;
But worse was to come in the concrete yard;
For the playground had split like a pastry crust,
And out of the clouds of smoke and dust,
Just like a curtain being parted,
And lit by the fires the bomb had started,
Unharmed in the heat that was blistering ...
Came a huge and shapeless, lumbering thing.

The boys in a heap were horrified;
Their mouths were open, their eyes were wide.
'It's as tall as two men!' 'As big as a bus!'
'It's heading this way!' 'It's coming for us!'
(Though a half-cheering thought did occur to Sid:
That'll show Simesy – he owes us a quid!)
Forgetting their bruises, ignoring the heat,
They frantically scrambled to their feet;
Fred, Denis, Albert; Timmy, Sid, Stan,
And like hares from the hounds they turned and ran.

Well, five of them ran, but one of them hobbled:
'Me ankle!' cried Stan. 'I'm gonna get gobbled!'
Five of them ran and four went free,
But Sid came back: 'Here, lean on me!'
And all the while at a lumbering pace,
The thing with the terrible hairy face
Advanced through the smoke – it was getting clearer –
With arms outstretched, coming nearer and nearer.

Then Sid 'n' Stan in desperate flight
Saw just ahead a welcome sight:
The toilets – still standing – untouched by the blaze
(School toilets were outside in those days).
Sid kicked at the door, they staggered inside,
It was really the only place to hide.
But the toilets, though solid, weren't due to last;
For while missing the blaze they had caught the blast;
And as Sid 'n' Stan crouched low on the floor,
The door slamming shut was the final straw.
(There are times in your life when you just can't win.)
Then the roof collapsed and the walls caved in.

In the few split seconds before he fainted,
Sid thought of his rabbit hutch – recently painted;
And his rabbit, a present from Uncle Clive,
And his rotten luck, being buried alive.
Stan's final thought was the pile of bricks
That fell on his head and knocked him for six.

Meanwhile, nearby a witness stood,
Observing the jumble of roof-tiles and wood;
A hairy witness, twelve feet high,
And black against the blazing sky.
It lumbered closer, and fell to its knees,
Then with hands like shovels and arms like trees,
And a body unbelievably big,
It set to work and began ... to dig.
(And the question is this: what would *you* choose,
In a situation where you're bound to lose?
Buried alive or dug up and ... well,
You see what I mean; it's hard to tell.)

Now the creature was quick, not to mention strong,
So the business of digging didn't take long.
It tossed aside roof-beams and toilet doors
(Disregarding its splintered paws),
Scooped armfuls of rubble from the pile
And glanced around just once in a while.
It cocked its head at the slightest noise,
And by-and-by it uncovered the boys.

Stan sensed a movement and heard a sound;
His eyelids fluttered, he began to come round.
He felt himself rising up into space;
Something hairy was brushing his face.
A mighty breath was on his cheek;
He opened his mouth but failed to speak.
He opened his eyes and looked about,
And saw his friend being lifted out.

Sid lay on his back in the bombed-out yard,
With his trousers torn and his eyebrows charred.
'I saw' (he said later) 'this horrible mug –
A mouth like a coal-hole, a face like a rug.
I thought – this is it – I've had it – Amen.
And then after that, well ... I fainted again.'

Which simply left Stan to report what occurred,
Though his thoughts were confused and his vision blurred.
('My eyes was watering from the smoke,
My ankle busted and my collarbone broke!')
So could he have seen what he said he saw,
As he sat in a daze on the playground floor?
A look of *concern* on that monstrous face,
When it lowered Sid to his resting place?
A gleam of *intelligence* in those eyes
Of preposterous blue and preposterous size?
And did he hear what he claimed he heard
(Though his ears were ringing and his *hearing* blurred)?
Its voice, and the two words: 'Than 'n' Thid'?
Well, decide for yourself, but *I* think he did.

The final scene a little while later,
With the school a quietly smouldering crater,
The steaming puddles, the sizzling snow
(Which had started to fall just a minute ago),
Showed Sid (unconscious) and Stan (unafraid)
Being 'rescued' by the fire brigade.

'Now then, young fella,' a fireman said,
'We'll soon have you tucked in a cosy bed.'
Stan tried to point and struggled to speak,
But his throat was parched and his arm was weak.
So the fireman failed to understand,
And never saw the massive hand
Raised (in a wave?) at the edge of the night,
As something huge passed out of sight.

It was dark in the classroom,
Dark everywhere
As the fog pressed up to the glass.
The teacher sighed deeply
And slumped in his chair,
And stared at the silent class.

'Did it ever come back?' the children cried.
(Their silence was short and sweet.)
'Did it walk the streets at the dead of night
On its huge and hairy feet?'
'Did it look in somebody's window, perhaps,
And wish their home was its?'
'Did it creep up somebody's stairs, perhaps,
And scare somebody to bits?'

'No, it never came back,' said the teacher;
'At least as far as I know.
Come on, now, let's have y'chairs up,
That's it – it's time to go.

'And I'll tell you another tomorrow,
One that you'll never forget;
For its horribly strange (as always),
And quite the scariest yet.

'I'll call it The Boy and the Blob, perhaps,
Or The Terror of Timbuctoo;
And remember, it's swimming on Friday;
Off you go now – home time – shoo!'